Mammal Inventory of Craters of the Moon National Monument and Preserve 2003

Upper Columbia Basin Network

Natural Resource Technical Report NPS/UCBN/NRTR—2009/272

Erica Madison
University of Idaho
Department of Fish and Wildlife Resources
Moscow, Idaho 83844-1136

Thomas J. Rodhouse
National Park Service, Upper Columbia Basin Network
Central Oregon Community College, 2600 NW College Way – Ponderosa Building
Bend, OR 97701-5998

Lisa K. Garrett
National Park Service, Upper Columbia Basin Network
University of Idaho, Department of Fish and Wildlife
Moscow, ID 83844-1136

November 2009

U.S. Department of the Interior
National Park Service
Natural Resource Program Center
Fort Collins, Colorado

The National Park Service, Natural Resource Program Center publishes a range of reports that address natural resource topics of interest and applicability to a broad audience in the National Park Service and others in natural resource management, including scientists, conservation and environmental constituencies, and the public.

The Natural Resource Technical Report Series is used to disseminate results of scientific studies in the physical, biological, and social sciences for both the advancement of science and the achievement of the National Park Service mission. The series provides contributors with a forum for displaying comprehensive data that are often deleted from journals because of page limitations.

All manuscripts in the series receive the appropriate level of peer review to ensure that the information is scientifically credible, technically accurate, appropriately written for the intended audience, and designed and published in a professional manner. This report received informal peer review by subject-matter experts who were not directly involved in the collection, analysis, or reporting of the data.

Views, statements, findings, conclusions, recommendations, and data in this report are those of the author(s) and do not necessarily reflect views and policies of the National Park Service, U.S. Department of the Interior. Mention of trade names or commercial products does not constitute endorsement or recommendation for use by the National Park Service.

This report is available from available from the Upper Columbia Basin Network website (http://www.nature.nps.gov/im/units/UCBN) and the Natural Resource Publications Management website (http://www.nature.nps.gov/publications/NRPM).

Please cite this publication as:

NPS 131/100701, November 2009

Contents

Figures

Tables

Executive Summary

The mission of the National Park Service is "to conserve unimpaired the natural and cultural resources and values of the national park system for the enjoyment of this and future generations" (National Park Service 1999). To uphold this goal, the Director of the NPS approved the Natural Resource Challenge to encourage national parks to focus on the preservation of the nation's natural heritage through science, natural resource inventories, and expanded resource monitoring (National Park Service 1999). Through the Challenge, 270 parks in the national park system were organized into 32 inventory and monitoring networks.

The 2003 Craters of the Moon mammal inventory contributed new information to the existing vertebrate species list for the Craters of the Moon National Monument and Preserve in southeast Idaho. The 2003 inventory built on previous mammal work conducted in the park in recent years. The University of Idaho Department of Fish and Wildlife Resources conducted the 2003 inventory under a cooperative agreement with the National Park Service Northern Semi-Arid Network (now the Upper Columbia Basin Network—UCBN) in partial fulfillment of the first phase of the Natural Resource Challenge Inventory and Monitoring program. Inventory fieldwork was conducted from May 20-June 27, 2003. The primary goal of the inventory was to confirm 90% of the species expected to occur in the monument and preserve. Additional goals included developing baseline data for monitoring as well as providing the National Park Service and the research community-at-large with new and important information on the biodiversity of the region.

Expected species lists were developed from published literature, available historical sources, expert opinion, and previous fieldwork. A set of four criteria was used to determine the likelihood of detection in the reserve. Fieldwork in 2003 utilized a variety of methods to achieve the primary objective, including visual encounter surveys and trapping. Species documentation included the collection of voucher photographs, specimens, digital bat call recordings, and field observation records.

The 2003 mammal inventory was productive and brought mammal species confirmation to 81%. Between the period 1990-2003, 45 species of mammals have been documented in or adjacent to the monument. One of those, the river otter (*Lutra canadensis*), was documented for the first time during the 2003 inventory. The moose (*Alces alces*), first documented in 1999, was observed in the monument at a greater rate in 2003 by monument and inventory staff. The deer mouse (*Peromyscus maniculatus*) and the Ord's kangaroo rat (*Dipodomys ordii*) were the two most abundant species captured during inventory efforts in 2003.

Data from the 2003 inventory is incorporated into an existing natural resource database at the monument and preserve, as well as the National Park Service Inventory and Monitoring NPSspecies database. This information is also available as "baseline" information for future vital signs monitoring. Future monitoring activities will also provide opportunities to add additional species to the inventory list as they are encountered.

Acknowledgements

The 2003 Craters of the Moon National Monument and Preserve mammal inventory was made possible through a cooperative agreement between the National Park Service Northern Semi-Arid Inventory and Monitoring Network (now the Upper Columbia Basin Network—UCBN) and University of Idaho Department of Fish and Wildlife Resources. We would like to extend a special thanks to Dr. Gerry Wright, USGS Idaho Cooperative Wildlife Research Unit and John Apel, Chief of Resource Management for the monument, for providing leadership, direction, and enthusiasm for the project. We are also indebted to the Craters of the Moon staff for providing support and contributing natural history sightings to us. Michael Munts, monument biologist, was particularly helpful with the project. Dr. Leon Powers, of Northwest Nazarene University, provided training and materials. Dr. Janet Rachlow and her graduate students from the University of Idaho provided training on pygmy rabbit surveys.

Introduction

This report summarizes the results of the 2003 inventory of mammals, summarizes historic information, and contains brief accounts of each species present or expected to occur at Craters of the Moon National Monument and Preserve (CRMO). Information on species that are possible but unlikely to occur at CRMO is also provided.

The University of Idaho Department of Fish and Wildlife Resources conducted the 2003 mammal inventory in CRMO under a cooperative agreement with the National Park Service Northern Semi-Arid Network (now the Upper Columbia Basin Network—UCBN). Inventory fieldwork was conducted from May 20 to June 27, 2003. The inventory is part of a nationwide inventory and monitoring (I & M) program initiated by the National Park Service Natural Resource Challenge. In 2000 the Northern Semi-Arid Network (UCBN), in which CRMO is part, began implementing the inventory phase of the I & M program in several network parks. Historic information available on the plant and animal populations within the network were assembled and an estimate was made of the percent of species expected to occur in each park. CRMO was among the majority of parks that had a low percentage (50%) of expected mammals documented and was in need of additional work to meet the I & M goal. The 2003 inventory built on existing mammal information developed by monument staff during recent years. The 2003 mammal inventory completes the biological inventory portion of the I & M program in CRMO. Previous inventories conducted in CRMO include an extensive bird inventory conducted by monument staff, herpetological inventory conducted by John Lee of Idaho State University in 2000-2002, and a plant inventory completed in 2003 by Steve Popovich of Wild Horse Consulting.

The primary goal of the inventory phase of the I & M program is to document the presence of 90% of the plant and animal species expected to occur within the park boundary or within a distance to the boundary that is relevant to the biology of the organism and to park management. Secondary goals on the inventory include providing baseline information that will help guide the development of the I & M program's vital signs monitoring strategy. Tertiary goals include providing both NPS and the research community-at-large new information on the distribution, habitat association, and population status of the nation's biological resources. Ultimately, the I & M program is designed to help NPS take a leading role in the preservation of the nation's biological diversity. Completing basic biological inventories is a crucial first step in achieving that goal.

Study Area

Craters of the Moon National Monument and Preserve (CRMO) is located on the northern edge of the eastern Snake River Plain of Idaho, in Lincoln, Minidoka, Blaine, Power, and Butte counties (Figure 1). The original monument was established in 1924 and included 53,440 acres. In 2000, an additional 661,000 acres was added to the existing monument as National Preserve land and is cooperatively managed by the National Park Service and the Bureau of Land Management (BLM). CRMO manages 415,000 acres of this new preserve.

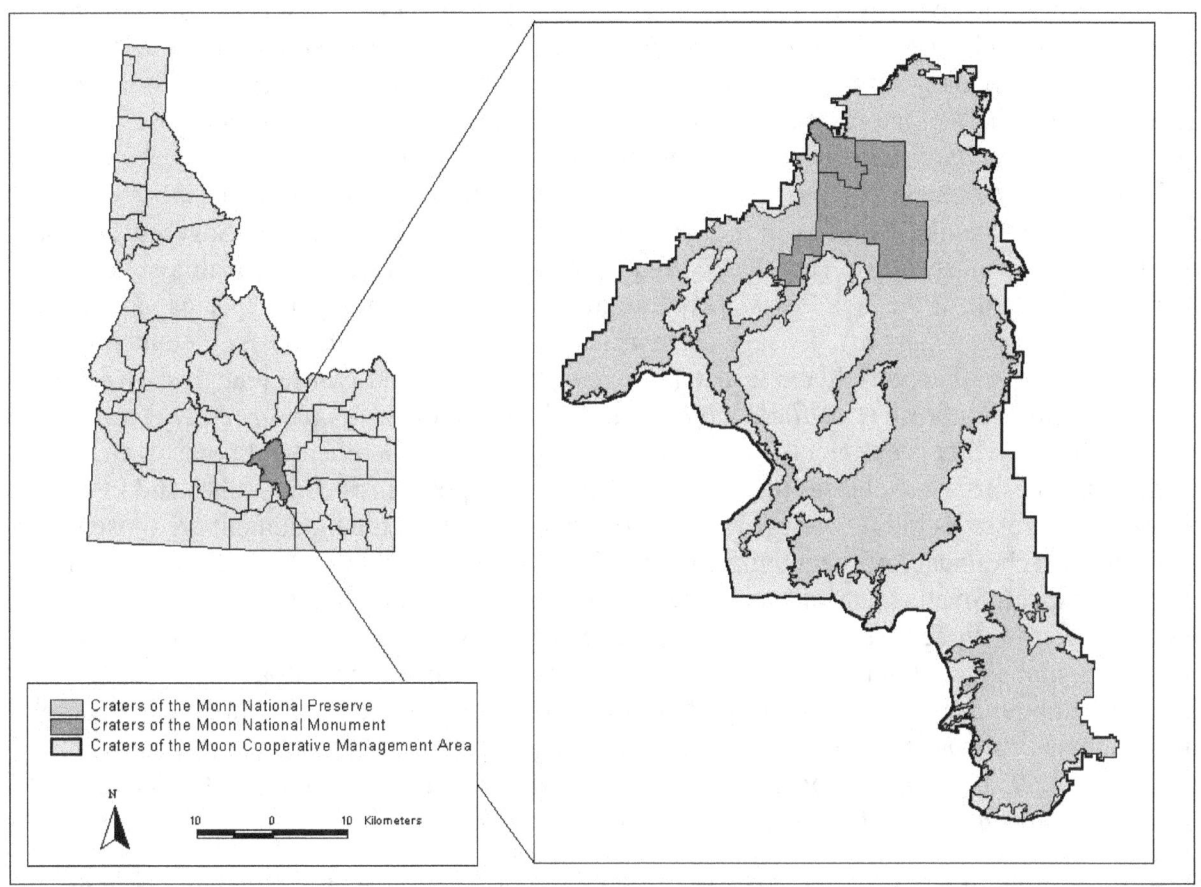

Figure 1. Map of the Craters of the Moon National Monument and Preserve.

This large area consists of a rugged landscape of volcanic lava flows and sagebrush steppe. During the last 15,000 years, molten basalt has periodically flowed from the Great Rift, a 50-mile long volcanic rift zone that lies within the monument. Lava fields encompass over 450,000 acres of the monument, and include 60 lava flows and 25 cinder cones. Sagebrush steppe makes up the approximately 250,000 remaining acres, much of which exists as islands within the lava flows, known as "kipukas".

CRMO runs from the foothills of the Pioneer Mountains south nearly to the Snake River. The monument rises from approximately 5330 ft. in the southern tip to 7729 ft. in the north. The climate is semi-arid, with hot and dry summers and cold and dry winters. Winter snows comprise most of the annual precipitation in the monument, especially in the north. Snow pack usually lasts most of the winter. The 30-year mean annual precipitation is 15 inches (CRMO weather station data). The average July maximum temperature is 84 $^{\circ}$F and average January minimum temperature is 10 degrees $^{\circ}$F (CRMO weather station data). Surface temperatures on the lava flows can reach 170 $^{\circ}$F during summer heat and winter temperatures frequently remain below freezing for long periods.

Craters of the Moon supports several different vegetation types. The harsh and barren environment of the lava flows support an unusual variety of plant communities. Spring forbs include dwarf buckwheat (*Eriogonum. ovalifolium var. depressum*), silverleaf phacelia (*Phacelia hastata*), dwarf monkey flower (*Mimulus nanus*), dwarf onion (*Allium parvum*) and bitterroot (*Lewisia rediviva*). Common shrubs include tansy bush (*Chamaebatiaria millefolium*), ocean spray (*Holodiscus dumosus*), dwarf goldenweed (*Haplopappus nanus*), bitterbrush (*Purshia tridentata*), and mountain big sage (*Artemisia. tridentata ssp. vaseyana*). On the slopes of cinder cones with deeper soils, stands of limber pine (*Pinus flexilis*) have developed. Sagebrush steppe vegetation is the most widespread plant community in the monument, growing almost everywhere outside of the lava flows, including the kipukas. Common plant species include three tip sage (*Artemisia tripartita*), big sage (*Artemisia. tridentata ssp. tridentata*), bluebunch wheat grass (*Agropyron spicatum*), Idaho fescue (*Festuca idahoensis*) and prairie junegrass (*Koeleria nitida*). Scarlet paintbrush (*Castilleja miniata*) and silvery lupine (*Lupinus argenteus*) are common forbs. Water is extremely scarce in the monument. Small ephemeral pools form during rainfall and subsurface ice lenses maintain small seeps and pools inside lava tubes and in the bottom of depressions in lava flows. The only riparian habitats in the monument are those found in the northern boundary of the monument where the lava flows and the foothills of the Pioneer Mountains meet. Small stands of aspen (*Populus tremuloides*) and Douglas' fir (*Pseudotsuga menzieseii*) grow along these slopes and several semi-permanent streams flow off the mountains into the monument. A 4-acre lake and a small hot springs complex exist along highway 20 near the northern boundary and provide important sources of water. Vegetation along these riparian areas includes cow parsnip (*Heracleum lanatum*), stinging nettle (*Urtica dioica*), small leaf angelica (*Angelica pinnata*), blackhead coneflower (*Rudbeckia occidentalis*), nettle leaf horsemint (*Agastache urticifolia*), and Sitka columbine (*Aquilegia formosa*).

Many species of introduced exotic vegetation have become established in the monument during recent decades. Cheatgrass (*Bromus tectorum*) and other plants have replaced native species in many areas and this has become a dominant resource management issue for the monument. Leafy spurge (*Euphorbia esula*), knapweeds (*Centaurea spp.*), rush skeleton weed (*Lygodesmia juncea*), and thistles (*Cirsium spp.*) have been documented in the monument. Of particular concern is the degree to which weeds are becoming established in the kipukas. Many of the kipukas have remained undisturbed from grazing, roads, and other sources of introduced weeds. While weeds are likely having a significant impact on mammal and other vertebrate populations in the monument, this impact has not been quantified in any way.

Methods

The methods utilized in the 2003 inventory generally follow those laid out in the Northern Semi-Arid Network (UCBN) Study Plan (Wright et al. unpublished) and published literature on inventory methodologies (i.e., Wilson et al. 1996). Universal Transverse Mercator (UTM) locations given in this report were collected using Garmin 12-channel Etrex hand-held GPS units (Garmin International, Inc, Olathe, KS, USA). Most x and y coordinates (Eastings and Northings) are accurate within 10 meters. No accuracy estimate is available for elevation data provided by the GPS unit. Locations taken directly from BLM topographic maps are accurate within approximately 125 meters. UTM locations are in zone 12 and the North American Datum of 1927 (NAD 27) was used as the horizontal datum for all locations.

Scientific and common names used in this report follow the Integrated Taxonomic Information System (ITIS). The ITIS follows closely the USGS Biological Resource Division's unpublished and expanded update of the 1987 Checklist of Vertebrates of the United States, the U.S. Territories, and Canada (ITIS 2003).

The monument and preserve boundaries were used as the primary boundaries of the inventory; however, species observed near the monument and preserve were also included. Flexibility in the boundary was necessary because dispersal abilities of many of the species enable them to move on and off the monument and preserve.

Expected Species

An expected mammal species list was provided by monument staff for use with this inventory. The list was refined somewhat, in order to meet the needs of the I & M program, by examining published range maps and species accounts, and consulting with regional experts. Range, elevation, habitat, and species detectability were considered and developed into a criteria set that was used to place species into "expected" or "possible but not expected" categories. Detectability was included in the consideration in order to address species that naturally occur in low abundances or are in some way very difficult to confirm through established mammal survey protocols. Species that met all four criteria were included as "expected" species. Monument staff have been assembling a species list over the course of several years and observations from 1990 to present were accepted as documentation of the species presence in the monument. Observations prior to 1990 are considered historic and were considered in the process of determining expected species.

Published sources used to determine the range, habitat, and elevation requirements of mammal species in the monument included *Mammals of Idaho* (Larrison 1981), *Land Mammals of Oregon* (Verts and Carraway 1998), *Mammals of the Rocky Mountains* (Pattie, Fisher, and Hartson 2000), *Ground Squirrels of the Pacific Northwest* (Yensen and Sherman 2003), and the *Digital Atlas of Idaho* (2003). Several unpublished reports from previous investigations on mammals in the monument were also examined, including a series of reports on bats in the monument (Keller and Saathoff 1995; Keller 1997) and numerous observations made by monument staff and visitors.

Sampling Site Selection

A subjective, non-random sampling site selection procedure was adopted for the inventory. This approach was determined to be the most efficient and effective given the primary objective of the inventory and the limited number of field personnel. Specific habitats and locations were identified and targeted for sampling in order to maximize the opportunities to encounter as many previously undocumented species as possible. The landscape in the monument is extremely rugged and a majority of the inventory effort was concentrated near roads and trails due to logistical considerations.

Visual Encounter Surveys

The visual encounter surveys and incidental observations were important tools in the mammal inventory. Visual encounter surveys were conducted by methodically searching target habitats. Visual surveys were done early in the morning and at night using flashlights. Incidental observations made of the mammals in or near CRMO during travel and other inventory activities were included. These observations contributed significantly to the overall success of the inventory and enabled participation from volunteers and NPS staff. Ancillary information recorded during visual encounter surveys included age, time, location, habitat, and notes of interest.

Road Surveys

Road surveys were conducted in the mammal inventory. Road surveys were conducted in the south part of CRMO early in the morning or late in the evenings when the weather was conducive. Because the monument is so large, road surveys allowed a single observer to cover large parts of the monument in a relatively small amount of time.

Trapping

A variety of trapping techniques were used to inventory small mammals and bats and generally followed procedures outlined in Jones et al. (1996), Cooperrider et al. (1986), Kunz (1988), and the Northern Semi-Arid Network (UCBN) Study Plan. Capture and handling procedures were consistent with those outlined by the Ad Hoc Committee on Acceptable Field Methods in Mammalogy (1987) and the University of Idaho Institutional Animal Care and Use Committee.

Small Mammals

The primary technique used for small mammals involved the use of Sherman live traps and Museum Special snap traps placed along 150-meter transects. Trap stations were established approximately every 15 meters and 2 traps were placed at each station. Both pre-baited and non pre-baited traps were set for four consecutive trap nights. Traps were placed within 2 meters of the transect center and were placed non-randomly near microhabitat features and mammal sign in order to maximize capture success. Traps were baited with peanut butter, crimped oats, and black oil sunflower seeds.

Miscellaneous trapping techniques included the use of Havahart wire cage traps targeted for skunks and weasels, and Museum Special snap traps baited for shrews with liver paste and placed near water. Ancillary data collected with small mammal captures included time, date, location, weather, moon phase, topography, age, sex, and habitat.

Bats

One night of mist netting was conducted on August 10, 2003 at the hot springs along Highway 20. Mist netting followed methods outlined in Kunz (1988). One 9-meter and 1 6-meter mist net designed specifically for bats (i.e., 38 mm mesh size with reduced bag) was placed over the main pool of the hot spring in an attempt to capture bats coming down to drink and to forage. Nets were opened at sunset and kept open until bat activity declined significantly, at 10:30 pm. Ancillary data collected with bat captures included time of capture, date, location, weather, time of sunset, moon phase, age, sex, reproductive condition, forearm length, and habitat. An *Anabat* bat echolocation call recording and analysis system (Titley Electronics, Ballina, NSW, Australia; Corben Scientific, Rohnert, CA, USA) was used to record and analyze the ultrasonic calls emitted by bats during foraging and drinking over Lava Lake. The *Anabat* system consisted of an *Anabat II* bat detector, type 6 standard Zero-Crossings Analysis Interface Mondule, an IBM-compatible laptop computer, and *Anabat 6* and *Analook* software. The *Anabat* system was setup along the southern shore of Lava Lake on a narrow peninsula that allowed the bat detector to be placed as close to the central portion of the lake as possible. *Anabat* was run on August 10, 2003, simultaneously to mist netting operations at the nearby hot springs. A 12-volt 100-watt handheld spotlight was used during recording sessions to illuminate flying bats and provide visual cues to aid in species identification. Species identification of free-flying bats was the primary application of the *Anabat*, although information on bat activity was also obtained from the use of *Anabat*. Recorded calls of bats were compared with an existing library of *Anabat* call files developed by releasing and recording bats captured and identified in the hand in other parks in the network. The library was used to enhance the species identification of calls recorded from free-flying bats. A set of voucher calls for each species documented with *Anabat* is included in Appendix B of this report (Figures B-1 and B-2).

Species Documentation Methods

Species encountered during the inventory were documented using digital photography, collections of voucher specimens, voucher *Anabat* call files, and field observation records. Mammals found dead on the road were also kept and skulls and study skins were prepared and provided to CRMO. Specimens not kept by CRMO are permanently housed at University of Washington's Burke Museum of Natural History in Seattle, Washington. Table 4, page 29, lists the species collected as voucher specimens during the 2003 inventory. Photocopies have been made of all data sheets and field notes and are permanently housed at the NPS Northern Semi-Arid Network (now the Upper Columbia Basin Network—UCBN) office in Moscow, ID.

Table 1. Voucher specimens collected in the monument during the 2003 mammal inventory.

Voucher No.	UTMX	UTMY	Date	Species
058tran05CRMO	290010	4818186	June 2, 2003	ZAPR
079tran05CRMO	290010	4818186	June 2, 2003	ZAPR

Results

Historic Information

While no comprehensive mammal inventory has been conducted in CRMO, several inventory efforts have been made in the past and a substantial amount of effort has been made in recent years to assemble existing information from historical sources, staff and visitor sightings, and trapping results from monument staff. Several collection expeditions were conducted in the park early in the 20th century and voucher specimens of many species are contained in museums around the country. Additional information on these specimens can be found in the NPS NPSpecies and ANCS+ databases (Blossom 1936). More recently, inventory projects were conducted by graduate students from Idaho State University and University of Idaho (Fuller 1969; Hoffman 1988). The presence of Townsend's big-eared bats (*Corynorhinus townsendii*) in the lava tube caves of the monument have attracted considerable research attention by researchers from Idaho State University and have provided many species confirmations for bats in the monument (Keller and Saathoff 1995; Keller 1997).

Expected and Confirmed Species

A total of 53 species of mammals are expected to occur in or adjacent to CRMO. Fourty-five species were documented from 1990 to 2003, one of which, the river otter, was not expected to occur in the park. Total confirmed expected species is 81%. Table 1 shows the list of expected and possible species and their current status in the monument inventory. (For the Species Account list refer to Appendix A).

Table 2. Confirmation status of expected and possible mammal species at Craters of the Moon National Monument and Preserve (2003) (continued).

Common Name	Scientific Name	Expected	Confirmed
Masked Shrew	Sorex cinereus	0	0
Dusky Shrew	Sorex monticolus	1	1
Vagrant Shrew	Sorex vagrans	1	0
Merriam's Shrew	Sorex merriami	0	0
Little Brown Myotis	Myotis lucifugus	1	1
Yuma Myotis	Myotis yumanensis	1	1
Long-eared Myotis	Myotis evotis	1	1
Long-legged Myotis	Myotis volans	1	1
Western Small-footed Myotis	Myotis ciliolabrum	1	1
Fringed Myotis	Myotis thysanodes	1	1
California Myotis	Myotis californicus	0	0
Silver-haired Bat	Lasionycteris noctivagans	1	0
Big Brown Bat	Eptesicus fuscus	1	1
Hoary Bat	Lasiurus cinereus	1	0
Townsend's Big-eared Bat	Corynorhinus townsendii	1	1
Pallid Bat	Antrozous pallidus	1	1
Pika	Ochotona princeps	1	1
Nuttall's Cottontail	Sylvilagus nuttallii	1	1
Snowshoe Hare	Lepus americanus	1	1
White-tailed Jackrabbit	Lepus townsendii	1	1
Black-tailed Jackrabbit	Lepus californicus	1	0
Pygmy Rabbit	Brachylagus idahoensis	1	0

Table 2. Confirmation status of expected and possible mammal species at Craters of the Moon National Monument and Preserve (2003) (continued).

Common Name	Scientific Name	Expected	Confirmed
Least Chipmunk	Tamias minimus	1	1
Yellow-pine Chipmunk	Tamias amoenus	1	1
Yellow-bellied Marmot	Marmota flaviventris	1	1
Great Basin Ground Squirrel	Spermophilus mollis	1	0
Uinta Ground Squirrel	Spermophilus armatus	0	0
Columbian Ground Squirrel	Spermophilus columbianus	1	1
Golden-mantled Ground Squirrel	Spermophilus lateralis	1	1
Wyoming Ground Squirrel	Spermophilus elegans	0	0
Red Squirrel	Tamiasciurus hudsonicus	1	1
Northern Pocket Gopher	Thomomys talpoides	1	1
Idaho Pocket Gopher	Thomomys idahoensis	0	0
Great Basin Pocket Mouse	Perognathus parvus	1	1
Ord's Kangaroo Rat	Dipodomys ordii	1	1
Beaver	Castor canadensis	1	1
Western Harvest Mouse	Reithrodontomys megalotis	1	1
Deer Mouse	Peromyscus maniculatus	1	1
Northern Grasshopper Mouse	Onychomys leucogaster	1	0
Desert Woodrat	Neotoma lepida	0	0
Bushy-tailed Woodrat	Neotoma cinerea	1	1
Heather Vole	Phenacomys intermedius	0	0
Montane Vole	Microtus montanus	1	1
Long-tailed Vole	Microtus longicaudus	1	1
Sagebrush Vole	Lemmiscus curtatus	0	0
Muskrat	Ondatra zibethicus	0	0
Western Jumping Mouse	Zapus princeps	1	1
Porcupine	Erethizon dorsatum	1	1
Coyote	Canis latrans	1	1
Gray Wolf	Canis lupus	1	0
Red Fox	Vulpes vulpes	1	1
Kit Fox	Vulpes velox	0	0
Black Bear	Ursus americanus	1	1
Raccoon	Procyon lotor	1	1
Ermine	Mustela erminea	1	0
Long-tailed Weasel	Mustela frenata	1	1
River Otter	Lutra canadensis	0	1
Badger	Taxidea taxus	1	1
Spotted Skunk	Spilogale gracilis	1	0
Striped Skunk	Mephitis mephitis	1	1
Mountain Lion	Felis concolor	1	1
Bobcat	Lynx rufus	1	1
Elk	Cervus elaphus	1	1
Mule Deer	Odocoileus hemionus	1	1
Moose	Alces alces	1	1
Pronghorn	Antilocapra americana	1	1
Total		**54**	**45**
Total % Confirmed[a]			**0.81**

[a] One species, the river otter, was not expected and is not included in this total.

Mammal Trapping

Trapping effort for small and medium sized non-volant mammals totaled 1,162 trap nights. Sherman live traps and Museum Special snap traps placed in transects represent 98% of these trap nights, but Havahart wire cage traps, and funnel traps were also used and are included in this total. Total capture of non-volant mammals was 280 individuals. Deer mice were the most abundant mammals captured, representing 79% of all captures. The Ord's kangaroo rat was the second most abundant mammal captured, representing 9% of all captures. Table 2 shows the 2003 trap locations and trapping effort information and Table 3 shows the results from the 2003 mammal trapping effort. Figure 2 shows the location of transects and miscellaneous capture locations.

Table 3. Transect location, date, and trap nights for the 2003 mammal inventory.

Transect	Date	Legal Description	UTM X	UTM Y	Trap Nights	Trap Type
Tran001	May20-22	T1N R23E S31 SW1/4	0274810	4804921	88	Sherman
Tran002	May 28-30	T2N R25E S33 SE1/4	0298759	4823369	132	Sherman
Tran003	May 28-30	T2N R24E S27 NW1/4	0290646	4816754	12	Sherman
Tran004	May 28-31	T2N R24E S27 NW1/4	0290613	4816742	40	Sherman
Tran005	May 28-31	T2N R24E S22 SW1/4	0290010	4818186	40	Sherman
Tran006	June 1-6	T2N R24E S21 SE1/4	0290176	4818084	70	Snap
Tran007	June 2-6	T2N R24E S27 NE1/4	0290701	4817558	72	Sherman
Tran008	June 2-6	T1S R24E S19 NE1/4	0291737	4816576	80	Sherman
Tran009	June 16-20	T1S R24E S19 NE1/4	0286613	4799761	80	Sherman
Tran010	June 16-20	T1S R24E S19 NE1/4	0286671	4799876	80	Sherman
Tran011	June 16-20	T1S R24E S19 NE1/4	0286729	4799886	40	Sherman
Tran012	June 16-20	T8S R27E S2 NW1/4	0313391	4736546	80	Sherman
Tran013	June 23-27	T8S R27E S2 NW1/4	0313438	4736533	80	Sherman
Tran014	June 23-27	T8S R27E S2 NW1/4	0310408	4734000	80	Sherman
Tran015	June 23-27	T8S R27E S17 NW1/4	0310309	4733213	80	Sherman
Tran016	June 23-27	T8S R27E S22 SW1/4	0310122	4731543	80	Sherman
Havahart N	June 16-20	T1S R24E S19 NE1/4	0286729	4799886	16	Havahart
Havahart S	June 23-27	T8S R27E S2 NW1/4	0313438	4736533	12	Havahart
Total					**1,162**	

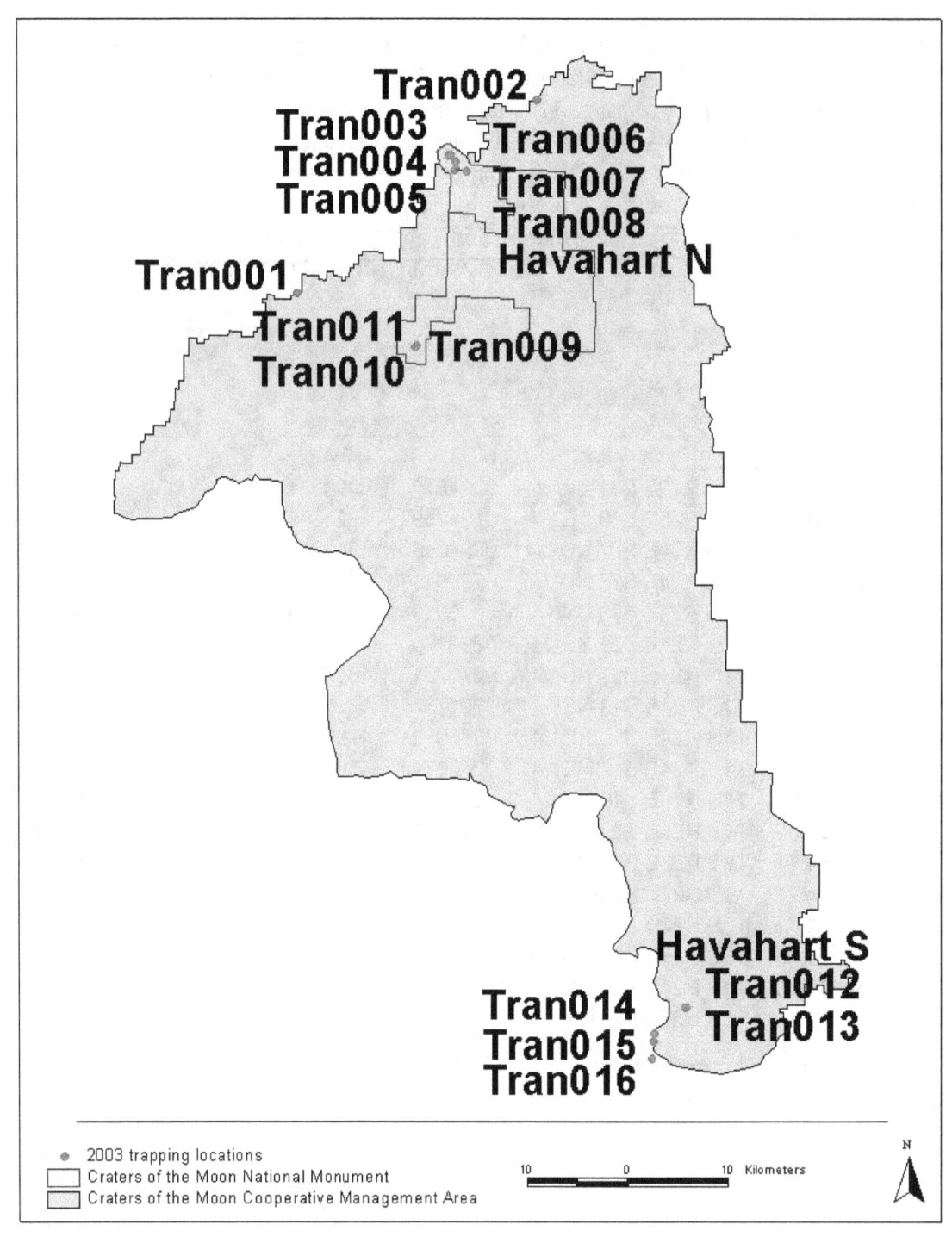

Figure 2. Location of trap transects in Craters of the Moon National Monument and Preserve during the 2003 mammal inventory.

Table 4. Trapping capture results of the 2003 mammal inventory[a].

Transect	PEMA	MIMO	PEPA	ZAPR	TAMI	DIOR	NECI	Total
Tran 001	22	1	0	0	0	0	0	23
Tran 002	20	8	0	0	0	0	0	28
Tran 003	2	0	2	0	0	0	0	4
Tran 004	3	0	0	4	0	0	0	7
Tran 005	0	0	0	0	0	0	0	0
Tran 006	15	0	0	3	0	0	0	18
Tran 007	27	0	0	0	0	0	0	27
Tran 008	22	0	4	0	3	0	0	29
Tran 009	12	0	2	0	0	0	0	14
Tran 010	14	0	0	0	0	0	0	14
Tran 011	8	0	0	0	2	0	0	10
Tran 012	12	0	1	0	0	0	0	13
Tran 013	18	0	0	0	0	0	2	20
Tran 014	19	0	0	0	0	0	0	19
Tran 015	6	0	1	0	0	8	0	15
Tran 016	5	0	0	0	0	9	0	14
Tran 017	17	0	0	0	0	8	0	25
Havahart (N)	4	0	2	0	0	0	0	6
Havahart (S)	2	0	1	0	0	0	2	5
Total	228	9	13	7	5	25	4	291
Relative Abundance	0.78	0.03	0.04	0.03	0.02	0.09	0.01	

[a] PEMA – *Peromyscus maniculatus*
MIMO – *Microtus montanus*
PEPA – *Perognathus parvus*
ZAPR – *Zapus princeps*

TAMI – *Tamias minimus*
DIOR – *Dipodomys ordii*
NECI – *Neotoma cinerea*

Bat Mist Netting

One mist net session was conducted on August 10, 2003. Far fewer bats were captured than expected. One female western small-footed myotis (*Myotis ciliolabrum*) and one female little brown myotis (*Myotis lucifugus*) were captured. Several other small myotis bats were seen flying in the area. Substantial mist netting was conducted during the 1990's by Idaho State University researchers that resulted in confirmation of almost all expected species of bats, including the two species captured in 2003.

Bat Acoustic Survey Results

Anabat recording was conducted simultaneously with mist netting on August 10, 2003. As with the level activity observed at the hot springs, overall bat activity at Lava Lake was surprisingly low. Only one call of the long-eared myotis (*Myotis evotis*) was recorded and the remaining calls were all made by unidentified species of myotis producing "40 Khz calls". Three species of myotis, all previously documented in the monument, produce similar calls that terminate at or near 40 Khz (O'Farrell et al. 1999). The little brown myotis, western small-footed myotis, and the long-legged myotis (*Myotis volans*) produce calls that are difficult to distinguish. The fact that all three species occur in the region precluded the ability to provide confident identifications from the calls recorded at Lava Lake on August 10th.

Discussion

The inventory work in 2003 at CRMO was based heavily upon past historic mammal information provided by the monument. Because a substantial number of expected species had already been confirmed prior to 2003, the number of new species documented in 2003 was limited. Nonetheless, the discovery of the river otter in the monument and reconfirmation of many other species were important additions to the vertebrate information database for the monument and preserve. The possibility that wolves may be ranging into the monument is also an important development. These new discoveries underscore the dynamic nature of mammal distributions and populations and illustrate the open-ended nature of the species lists generated through the I & M program. These lists will continue to be updated and refined as information from vital signs monitoring and other projects become available.

Shrews (family Soricidae) were a group of interest in the 2003 mammal inventory due to the lack of documentation after 1990. Of the two expected species, only the dusky shrew (*Sorex monticolus*) has been confirmed in CRMO. In 2003, efforts targeting vagrant shrews (*Sorex vagrans*) along the riparian areas in Little Cottonwood Canyon were made. The Merriam's shrew (*Sorex merriami*) may occur in the monument but the species is notoriously hard to capture and its habitat requirements are poorly known, making it difficult to effectively target this species (Kirkland et al 1997; Verts and Carraway 1998). Shrews in general are a poorly known group in Idaho and any future information collected on the family in CRMO will make a significant contribution to the understanding of their ecology and conservation (Digital Atlas of Idaho 2003). The dusky and vagrant shrews are difficult to differentiate and must be collected for identification under laboratory conditions and preserved as voucher specimens.

The Ord's kangaroo rat was rediscovered during the 2003 inventory in the southern portion of the monument near the Snake River. This species had been documented in the monument prior to 1990. The species was relatively common in suitable habitat and represented a large proportion of captures in 2003. Kangaroo rats were most common in sandy soils with a large component of perennial bunchgrasses and rabbitbrush (*Chrysothamnus spp.*).

The river otter was a surprising discovery in 2003. This species was not expected to occur in the monument because of the lack of significant water bodies. The animal was found dead along Highway 20 and was presumably a dispersing individual. It was found several miles away from Lava Lake and may have come from the Wood River, west of the monument.

Bats have been well studied in the monument during the 1990's. Idaho State University researchers investigated bat use of lava tubes and conducted mist-netting efforts along Little Cottonwood Creek. The Townsend's big-eared bat (*Corynorhinus townsendii*), a federal species of concern, was shown to utilize several caves in the monument for hibernation and summer pup rearing. In 2003, the hot spring and Lava Lake, both along Highway 20, were targeted for bat work because neither site had apparently been included in past research. Two expected species of bats, the hoary bat (*Lasiurus cinereus*) and silver-haired bat (*Lasionycteris noctivagans*), remain to be documented in the park and these sites, especially Lava Lake, should provide important foraging and drinking resources for those species. The low level of bat activity at those sites on August 10th was surprising. The weather preceding and during the survey period was warm and calm. The lack of water in the area outside of these two sites is such that these should be magnets for bats. Because so many Idaho bat species are listed as state or federal species of concern, and because previous work has shown that CRMO provides important resources for bats, future monitoring efforts should include this group of unique vertebrates.

The pygmy rabbit is another important species of concern that may be present in the monument. The Columbia Basin subpopulation, endemic to eastern Washington and western Idaho, was recently listed as a threatened species under the Endangered Species Act. While the sagebrush habitat favored by this species is abundant in the monument, it is not entirely clear whether all habitat components, such as soil characteristics, are present. Future monitoring efforts should be made to better assess the status of the species in the monument as well as habitat suitability. Monument staff should be encouraged to learn how to differentiate pygmy rabbit sign from that of the mountain cottontail (*Sylvilagus nuttallii*) in order to avoid misidentification.

Literature Cited

Ad hoc Committee on Acceptable Field Methods in Mammalogy. 1987. Acceptable field methods in mamalogy: preliminary guidelines approved by the American Society of Mammalogists. Journal of Mammalogy 68(4) supplement: 18 pp.

Blossom, P. M. 1936. A provisional list of mammals, Craters of the Moon, Idaho.

Cooperrider, A. Y., R. J. Boyd, and H. R. Stuart. 1986. Inventory and monitoring of wildlife habitat. U.S. Dept. of Interior Bureau of Land Management Service Center. Denver, Colorado.

Digital Atlas of Idaho. 2003. Digital atlas of Idaho: Idaho's natural history online. Idaho Museum of Natural History. Idaho State University, Pocatello, Idaho. Online. (http://imnh.isu.edu/digitalatlas). Accessed 23 October 2003.

Fuller, T. D. 1969. An ecological survey of the mammals of the Craters of the Moon National Monument. M.S. Thesis, Idaho State University, Pocatello, Idaho.

Groves, C. R., B. Butterfield, A. Lippincott, B. Csuti, and J .M. Scott. 1997. Atlas of Idaho's Wildlife. The Idaho Department of Fish and Game, The Nature Conservancy, & Idaho Gap Analysis Project, joint publishers.

Hoffman, R. A. 1988. Craters of the Moon National Monument baseline inventory and monitoring (wildlife). Final Report B–88-4: Cooperative Park Studies Unit, University of Idaho, Moscow, Idaho.

ITIS (Integrated Taxonomic Information System). 2003. Integrated taxonomic information system on-line database system. U.S. Department of Agriculture. Online. (http://www.itis.gov/). Accessed 1 October 2003.

Jones, C., W. J. McSea, M. J. Conroy, and T. H. Kunz. 1996. Capturing mammals. Pages 115–156 in D. E. Wilson, F. R. Cole, J. D. Nichols, R. Rudran, and M. S. Foster, editors. Measuring and monitoring biological diversity: standard methods for mammals. Smithsonian Institution Press, Washington D.C.

Keller, B. and R. T. Saathoff. 1995. A survey of day roosting by *Plecotus townsendii* in lava tube caves at Crater of the Moon National Monument, Butte County, Idaho. Idaho State University Museum of Natural History, Pocatello, Idaho.

Keller, B. 1997. Analysis of the thermal characteristics of maternity caves and bat species present at Craters of the Monument National Monument, Butte County, Idaho. Western Environmental Research Associates, Pocatello, Idaho.

Kirkland, G. L., Jr., R. R. Parmenter, and R. E. Skoog. 1997. A five-species assemblage of shrews from the sagebrush-steppe of Wyoming. Journal of Mammalogy 78(1):83–89.

Kunz, T. H., editor. 1988. Ecological and behavioral methods for the study of bats. Smithsonian Institution Press, Washington D.C.

Larrison, E. J. 1981. Mammals of Idaho. University Press of Idaho, Moscow, Idaho.

O'Farrell, M. J., B. W. Miller, and W. L. Gannon. 1999. Qualitative identification of free-flying bats using the Anabat detector. Journal of Mammalogy 80(1):11–23.

Pattie, D., Fisher, C., and P. T. Hartson. 2000. Mammals of the Rocky Mountains. Lone Pine Publishing, Renton, Washington.

Rachlow, J., and L. Scancava. 2003. Pygmy rabbit habitat in Idaho. University of Idaho Fish and Wildlife Resources and Landscape Dynamics Lab, Moscow, Idaho.

Verts, B. J., and L. N. Carraway. 1998. Land mammals of Oregon. University of California Press, Berkeley.

Wilson, D. E., F. R. Cole, J. D. Nichols, R. Rudran, and M. S. Foster. 1996. Measuring and monitoring biological diversity: Standard methods for mammals. Smithsonian Institution Press, Washington, D.C.

Wright, G. R., L. Garrett, and D. Foster. Unpublished. A study plan to inventory vascular plants and vertebrates in national park service units in the northern semi-arid network. University of Idaho Department of Fish and Wildlife. Moscow, Idaho.

Yensen, E. and P. W. Sherman. 2003. Ground dwelling squirrels of the Pacific Northwest. U.S. Fish and Wildlife Service, Snake River Fish and Wildlife Office. Boise, Idaho.

Appendix A. Species Accounts

This section gives a brief description of each expected or unexpected but possible species for CRMO. The mammals are divided into expected and unexpected species, but only unexpected species that have been confirmed are included. Species names are followed by a series of codes based on those in use by the National Park Service NPSpecies database (below). The first code indicates park status, followed by an indication of CRMO units in which the species has been observed, species abundance, and species residency.

NPSpecies Codes

Park Status
- **(P) Present**: Species occurrence in park is documented and assumed to be extant.
- **(H) Historic:** Species historical occurrence in the park is documented, but recent investigations indicate that the species is now probably absent.
- **(PP) Probably Present:** Park is within species range and contains appropriate habitat. Documented occurrences of the species in the adjoining region of the park give reason to suspect that it probably occurs within the park. The degree of probability may vary within this category, including species that range from common to rare.
- **(E) Encroaching**: The species is not documented in the park, but is documented as being adjacent to the park and has potential to occur in the park.
- **(U) Unconfirmed:** Included for the park based on weak (unconfirmed) record or no evidence, giving minimal indication of the species occurrence in the park.
- **(FR) False Report:** Species previously reported to occur within the park, but current evidence indicates that the report was based on a misidentification, a taxonomic concept no longer accepted, or some other similar problem of interpretation.

Species Abundance
- **(A) Abundant:** *May be seen daily, in suitable habitat and season, and counted in relatively large numbers.*
- **(C) Common:** *May be seen daily, in suitable habitat and season, but not in large numbers.*
- **(U) Uncommon:** *Likely to be seen monthly in appropriate season/habitat. May be locally common.*
- **(R) Rare:** *Present, but usually seen only a few times each year.*
- **(O) Occasional:** *Occurs in the park at least once every few years, but not necessarily every year. Applicable to animals only.*
- **(UNK) Unknown:** *Abundance unknown.*

Residency
- **(B) Breeder:** Population reproduces in the park.
- **(R) Resident:** A significant population is maintained in the park for more than two months each year, but it is not known to breed there.
- **(M) Migratory:** Migratory species that occurs in park approximately two months or less each year and does not breed there.
- **(V) Vagrant:** Park is outside of the species usual range.
- **(UNK) Unknown:** Residency status in park is unknown

Expected Species

Dusky Shrew (*Sorex monticolus*)   Present   R   B
This species was captured in a funnel trap set for reptiles in 2001 near Little Cottonwood Canyon.

Vagrant Shrew (*Sorex vagrans*)   Probably Present
An unvouchered brown shrew that may have been a vagrant shrew was captured in the monument prior to 1990. It likely occurs in riparian habitats along the northern tier of the monument.

Long-eared Myotis (*Myotis evotis*)   Present   C   B
This species has been documented in the monument during research conducted by Barry Keller, Idaho State University, during the 1990's. The species has been documented using lava tube caves in the monument. One call of this species was recorded at Lava Lake in 2003.

Little Brown Myotis (*Myotis lucifugus*)   Present   UNK   UNK
This species has been documented in the monument during research conducted by Barry Keller, Idaho State University, during the 1990's. One individual was captured at the hot springs in 2003.

Fringed Myotis (*Myotis thysanodes*)   Present   UNK   UNK
This species has been documented in the monument during research conducted by Barry Keller, Idaho State University, during the 1990's. This is an Idaho state species of concern.

Long-legged Myotis (*Myotis volans*)   Present   UNK   UNK
This species has been documented in the monument during research conducted by Barry Keller, Idaho State University, during the 1990's.

Yuma Myotis (*Myotis yumanensis*)   Present   UNK   UNK
This species has been documented in the monument during research conducted by Barry Keller, Idaho State University, during the 1990's.

Hoary Bat (*Lasiurus cinereus*)   Probably Present
This species is widespread in Idaho and probably occurs sporadically in the monument. The species is migratory and highly transient, but is found in other parks in the network and frequently occurs in habitat similar to the monument.

Silver-haired Bat (*Lasionycteris noctivagans*)   Probably Present
This species is widespread in Idaho and probably occurs sporadically in the monument. The species is migratory and highly transient, but is found in other parks in the network and frequently occurs in habitat similar to the monument.

Big Brown Bat (*Eptesicus fuscus*)   Present   UNK   UNK
This species has been documented in the monument during research conducted by Barry Keller, Idaho State University, during the 1990's.

Townsend's Big-eared Bat (*Corynorhinus townsendii*)
$$\text{Present} \qquad \text{C} \qquad \text{B}$$
This species has been documented in the monument during research conducted by Barry Keller, Idaho State University, during the 1990's. The species uses lava tubes in the monument as hibernacula and as summer maternity roosts. This is an Idaho state species of concern.

Pallid Bat (*Antrozous pallidus*)   Present   UNK   UNK
This species may be rare in the monument. It was documented in 2002 through an acoustic bat echolocation analysis system by a visitor.

Western Small-Footed Myotis (*Myotis ciliolabrum*)
$$\text{Present} \qquad \text{C} \qquad \text{B}$$
This species has been documented in the monument during research conducted by Barry Keller, Idaho State University, during the 1990's. This species occurs throughout the monument and uses lava tubes as day roosts. One female was captured at the hot springs in 2003.

Pika (*Ochotona princeps*)   Present   C   B
The pika occurs in the lava flow habitats of the northern portion of the monument.

Mountain Cottontail (Sylvilagus nuttallii)   Present   C   B
The mountain cottontail occurs throughout the monument.

Snowshoe Hare (*Lepus americanus*)   Present   U   B
This species occurs in the northern portion of the monument, especially along the foothills of the Pioneer Mountains.

White-tailed Jackrabbit (*Lepus townsendii*)   Present   R   UNK
This species was documented most recently along highway 20 near the northern boundary of the monument.

Black-tailed Jackrabbit (*Lepus californicus*)   Probably Present
This species is widespread in Idaho and has been documented in the monument prior to 1990. Its absence in the monument during recent years is conspicuous and may be a cause for concern.

Pygmy Rabbit (*Brachylagus idahoensis*)   Probably Present
A pygmy rabbit was reported crossing Highway 20 near the north end of the monument 2003. Historic records for the species exist prior to 1990 as well. Suitable habitat may be present in and around the monument (Rachlow and Svancava 2003). This species is listed as a species of concern by the state of Idaho and additional surveys should be conducted in the monument to assess the habitat and status of this species.

Least Chipmunk (*Tamias minimus*)   Present   C   B
This species is difficult to distinguish from the yellow-pine chipmunk. The two species were distinguished by pelage coloration and habitat. The least chipmunk occurs throughout the sagebrush habitat in the monument, including the visitor center.

Yellow-pine Chipmunk (*Tamias amoenus*)   Present   C   B

This species is difficult to distinguish from the least chipmunk. The two species were distinguished by pelage coloration and habitat. Yellow-pine chipmunks occur in the northern portion of the monument among stands of pine, fir, and aspen.

Yellow-bellied Marmot (*Marmota flaviventris*)   Present   C   B

The yellow-bellied marmot occurs in the northern part of the monument in and near lava tubes and large lava crevices that border sagebrush vegetation.

Great Basin Ground Squirrel (*Spermophilus mollis*)

Probably Present

This species has been documented in the monument in the past. The sagebrush steppe habitat throughout the monument is suitable for the species and it probably still occurs there but has not been confirmed recently.

Columbian Ground Squirrel (*Spermopholis columbianus*)

Present   U   B

This species occurs in the sagebrush steppe areas in the northern portion of the monument.

Golden-mantled Ground Squirrel (*Spermophilus lateralis*)

Present   A   B

This species is common in the north end of the park, especially near the visitor center.

Red Squirrel (*Tamiasciurus hudsonicus*)   Present   U   B

The red squirrel occurs in the northern part of the monument along Little Cottonwood Canyon, where an isolated stand of Douglas fir occurs within a larger stringer of aspen.

Northern Pocket Gopher (*Thomomys talpoides*)   Present   C   B

The northern pocket gopher occurs throughout the monument.

Great Basin Pocket Mouse (*Perognathus parvus*)   Present   A   B

This species was the second most common species captured during the 2003 inventory. It occurs throughout the sagebrush steppe habitats in the monument.

Ord's Kangaroo Rat (*Dipodomys ordii*)   Present   C   B

This species was captured in the southern portion of the monument in 2003, particularly in areas with sandy soils.

Beaver (*Castor canadensis*)   Present   UNK   UNK

This species occurs along riparian areas in the northern portion of the monument. The species was last seen in 1999 along Little Cottonwood Canyon. Recently, the species has been less visible in the area which may be a response to abnormally low surface flow in the creek.

Western Harvest Mouse (*Reithrodontomys megalotis*)

Present   C   B

The Western Harvest Mouse is found throughout the monument in sagebrush and grassland areas.

Deer Mouse (*Peromyscus maniculatus*)   Present   A   B
This ubiquitous species was the most abundant mammal captured in the 2003 inventory. It occurs throughout the monument.

Northern Grasshopper Mouse (*Onychomys leucogaster*)
                                                            Probably Present
This species is difficult to capture but suitable habitat is abundant in the monument, especially in the southern portion. Voucher specimens were collected in the monument in the 1920's.

Bushy-tailed Woodrat (*Neotoma cinerea*)   Present   C   B
This species occurs throughout the monument, especially in the lava flows and other rocky areas.

Montane Vole (*Microtus montanus*)   Present   U   B
The montane vole occurs near riparian areas of the park.

Long-tailed Vole (*Microtus longicaudus*)   Present   U   B
This species was not captured in 2003 but one was regularly observed using a hole in the outside wall of a staff house in the visitor center.

Western Jumping Mouse (*Zapus princeps*)   Present   U   B
The western jumping mouse occurs in the riparian area of Little Cottonwood Canyon.

Porcupine (*Erethizon dorsatum*)   Present   U   B
This mammal occurs throughout the monument, especially in the Aspen groves in the northern portion of the monument.

Coyote (*Canis latrans*)   Present   C   B
This ubiquitous species occurs throughout the monument.

Gray Wolf (*Canis lupus*)   Probably Present
Wolf scat and tracks have been recently reported near the northern boundary of the monument. The Idaho Department of Fish and Wildlife are currently radio tracking three gray wolves that may have territory overlapping the monument.

Red Fox (*Vulpes vulpes*)   Present   R   UNK
Red fox have been observed by some of the staff members of CRMO within the past five years. Most of the documentation has been along the northern boundary of the park, running along Highway 20. A road kill fox was found east of the town of Carey, approximately 10 miles from the monument, in August, 2003.

Black Bear (*Ursus americanus*)   Present   R   UNK
The black bear is infrequently encountered along the northern boundary of the monument. A monument employee sighted a bear in Little Cottonwood Canyon in 2001.

Common Raccoon (*Procyon lotor*)　　　　　　Present　　　　　　U　　UNK
A park intern saw a raccoon outside the park housing complex in August of 2003.

Ermine (*Mustela erminea*)　　　　　　Probably Present
This species is expected to occur along the riparian corridors in the northern boundary of the monument. The aspen and fir along Little Cottonwood Canyon is a particularly suitable area for the species. An historic report for this species exists in the monument prior to 1980.

Long-tailed Weasel (*Mustela frenata*)　　　　　　Present　　　　　　U　　B
The long tailed weasel probably occurs throughout the park, and is frequently seen in and around the visitor center.

American Badger (*Taxidea taxus*)　　　　　　Present　　　　　　U　　B
This species occurs throughout the monument, especially near ground squirrel colonies. Fresh and abandoned badger excavations and sign were encountered during the 2003 inventory and badgers were occasionally seen in the monument as well.

Western Spotted Skunk (*Spilogale gracilis*)　　　Probably Present
This species is secretive, but probably occurs in the monument. An historic report exists for the species in the monument prior to 1980.

Striped Skunk (*Mephitis mephitis*)　　　　　　Present　　　　　　O　　UNK
The striped skunk has been documented on several occasions during recent years in and near the monument. It has been documented through road kill and individuals have also been seen traveling along the roadside ditch of Highway 20.

Mountain Lion (*Felis concolor*)　　　　　　Present　　　　　　O　　UNK
Cougars are secretive and hard to document but presumed to occur periodically in the monument. Several reports of cougars have come from monument visitors and staff in recent years.

Bobcat (*Lynx rufus*)　　　　　　Present　　　　　　R　　B
Bobcats are infrequently seen in the monument but are secretive and may be more common than rare sightings indicate.

Elk (*Cervus elaphus*)　　　　　　Present　　　　　　R　　UNK
This species occurs in the northern part of the monument in the foothills of the Pioneer Mountains. Large herds assemble in the winter but are only seldom encountered.

Mule Deer (*Odocoileus hemionus*)　　　　　　Present　　　　　　C　　B
Mule deer are frequently encountered throughout the monument.

Moose (*Alces alces*)　　　　　　Present　　　　　　U　　UNK
The moose has only been documented in the northern part of the park, near Little Cottonwood Canyon, the Pioneer Mountains, and in Lava Lake.

Pronghorn (*Antilocapra americana*)   Present   C   UNK

Pronghorn occur in low numbers throughout the sagebrush and grassland habitats of the monument. Small herds are encountered at the base of the Pioneer Mountains and also in the central portion of the monument.

Unexpected Species

Masked Shrew (*Sorex cinereus*)
The monument is outside the range of this species and the species is generally found at higher elevations and in more extensive forest habitat than what is available in the monument (Larrison 1981; Digital Atlas of Idaho 2003).

Merriam's Shrew (*Sorex merriami*)
This species has not been documented in the monument. It is extremely difficult to capture and apparently occurs in naturally low abundances throughout its range (Kirkland et al 1997; Verts and Carraway 1998). The species may occur in the sagebrush habitat of the monument.

California Myotis (*Myotis californicus*)
While this species may occur in eastern Idaho, it has only been documented along the western border of the state (Digital Atlas of Idaho 2003).

Uinta Ground Squirrel (*Spermopholis armatus*)
This range of this species does not overlap with the monument (Digital Atlas of Idaho 2003, Yensen and Sherman 2003).

Wyoming Ground Squirrel (*Spermophilus elegans*)
The monument occurs on the periphery of the species' range (Digital Atlas of Idaho 2003; Yensen and Sherman 2003).

Idaho Pocket Gopher (*Thomomys idahoensis*)
Although this species may occur in the monument, its predicted range does not overlap with the monument (Larrison 1981; Digital Atlas of Idaho 2003).

Desert Woodrat (*Neotoma lepida*)
The monument is on the periphery of this species' range (Larrison 1981; Digital Atlas of Idaho 2003).

Heather Vole (*Phenacomys intermedius*)
This species is not expected to occur in the monument because it is on the periphery of the species predicted range (Digital Atlas of Idaho 2003). The species is normally found in higher elevation alpine habitats than what are available in the monument (Larrison 1981; Verts and Carraway 1998; Digital Atlas of Idaho 2003).

Sagebrush Vole (*Lemmiscus curtatus*)
This species is difficult to capture but may occur in the southern portion of the monument in low elevation sagebrush steppe.

Common Muskrat (*Ondatra zibethicus*)
This species may occur in riparian area near the monument but is not expected due to the lack of significant riparian habitat in the monument. The species was reported prior to 1980, but like the occurrence of the river otter in 2003, probably represents a rare event.

Kit Fox (*Vulpes velox*)
The monument is outside the range of this species (Larrison 1981; Verts and Carraway 1998; Digital Atlas of Idaho 2003). A historic report for the kit fox in the monument exists prior to 1990 but this may be a misidentification.

River Otter (*Lutra canadensis*)   Present   UNK   UNK
This species was found dead on the side of Highway 20, 2 miles west of Lava Lake. The closest significant watercourse is the Wood River, approximately five miles away. This is probably a rare event, possibly representing a dispersal attempt.

Appendix B. Bat Echolocation Figures

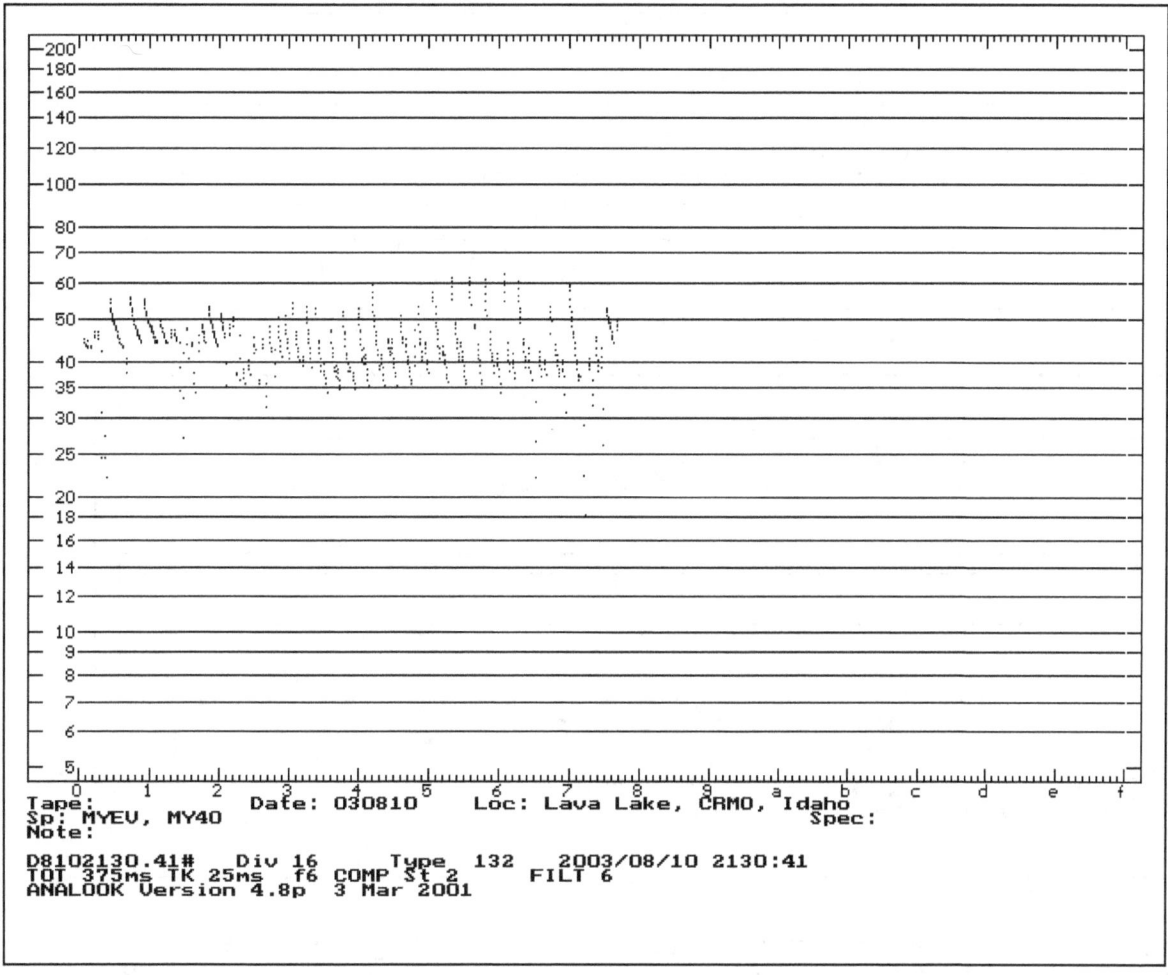

Figure B-1. A long-eared myotis echolocation call recorded at Lava Lake along the northern boundary of Craters of the Moon National Monument and Preserve.

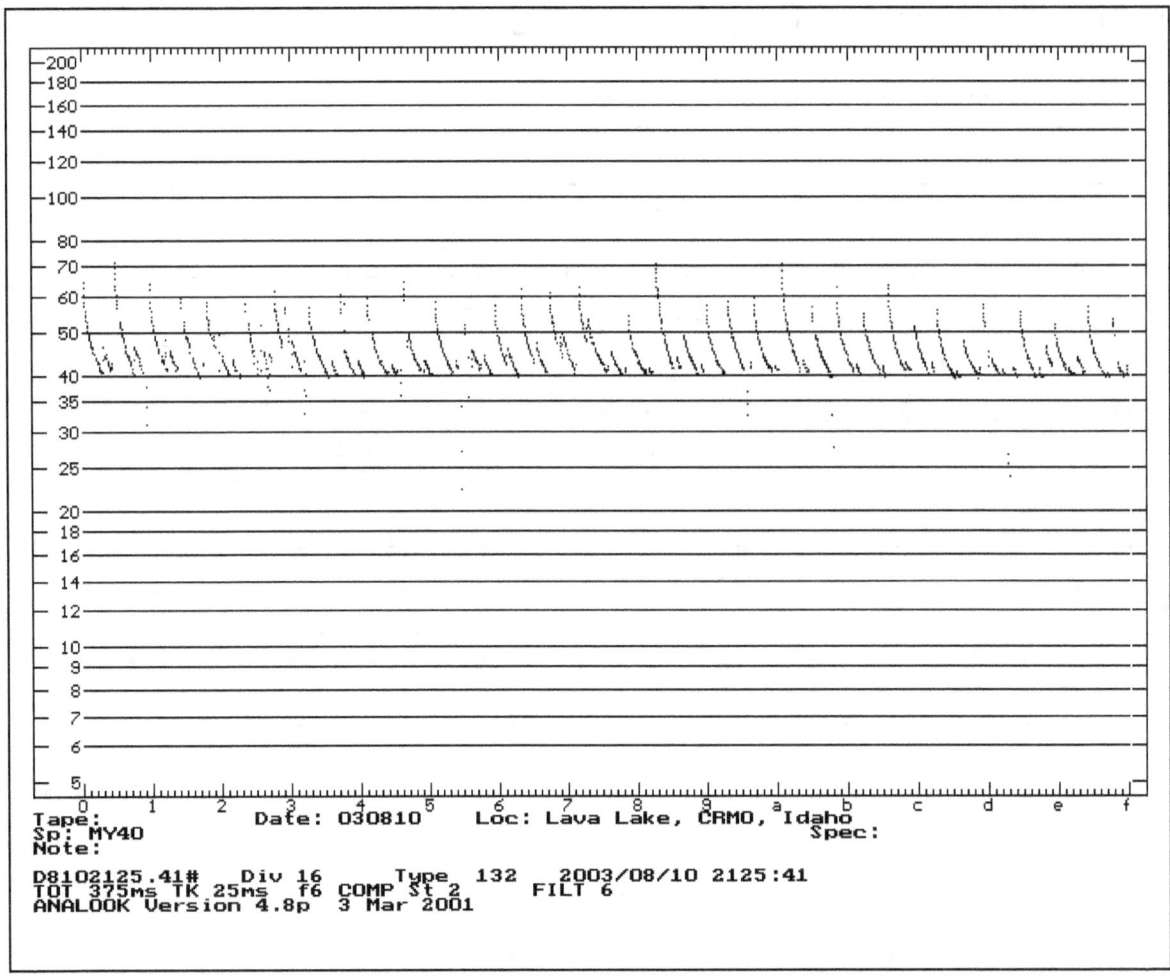

Figure B-2. A "40Khz myotis" echolocation call recorded at Lava Lake along the northern boundary of Craters of the Moon. This "40Khz" call was made by a little brown myotis (*Myotis lucifugus*), western small-footed myotis (*Myotis ciliolabrum*), or a long-legged myotis (*Myotis volans*).

The Department of the Interior protects and manages the nation's natural resources and cultural heritage; provides scientific and other information about those resources; and honors its special responsibilities to American Indians, Alaska Natives, and affiliated Island Communities.

NPS 131/100701, November 2009